THE CAMBRIDGESHIRE
COLOURING BOOK

First published 2017

The History Press
The Mill, Brimscombe Port
Stroud, Gloucestershire, GL5 2QG
www.thehistorypress.co.uk

British Library Cataloguing in Publication Data.
A catalogue record for this book is available from the British Library.

ISBN 978 0 7509 7997 9

Typesetting and origination by The History Press
Printed and bound in Great Britain by TJ International Ltd.

THE CAMBRIDGESHIRE
COLOURING BOOK

PAST AND PRESENT

Take some time out of your busy life to relax and unwind with this feel-good colouring book designed for everyone who loves Cambridgeshire.

Absorb yourself in the simple action of colouring in the scenes and settings from around the county, past and present. From iconic architecture to picturesque vistas, you are sure to find some of your favourite locations waiting to be transformed with a splash of colour.

There are no rules – choose any page and any choice of colouring pens or pencils you like to create your own unique, colourful and creative illustrations.

Bridge of Sighs, Cambridge ▸

King's Parade, Cambridge ▸

Hemingford Grey, *c.* 1900 ▸

King's College Chapel, Cambridge ▶

Cambridge tram, 1914 ▸

Oliver Cromwell's House, Ely ▸

Nene Valley Railway, Peterborough ▸

The Fitzwilliam Museum, Cambridge ▸

St Ives, Huntingdonshire ▶

Anglesey Abbey, Cambridge ▸

Trinity College, Cambridge ▶

Wicken Windmill ▸

Wimpole Estate, Arrington ▸

Trumpington Street, Cambridge, *c.* 1880 ▸

Houghton Mill, a watermill located on the Great Ouse in Houghton ▸

Bronze-Age dwelling at Flag Fen ▶

Ely Cathedral ▶

Spitfire N3200 at the Duxford Air Show ▸

Clare College, Cambridge ▶

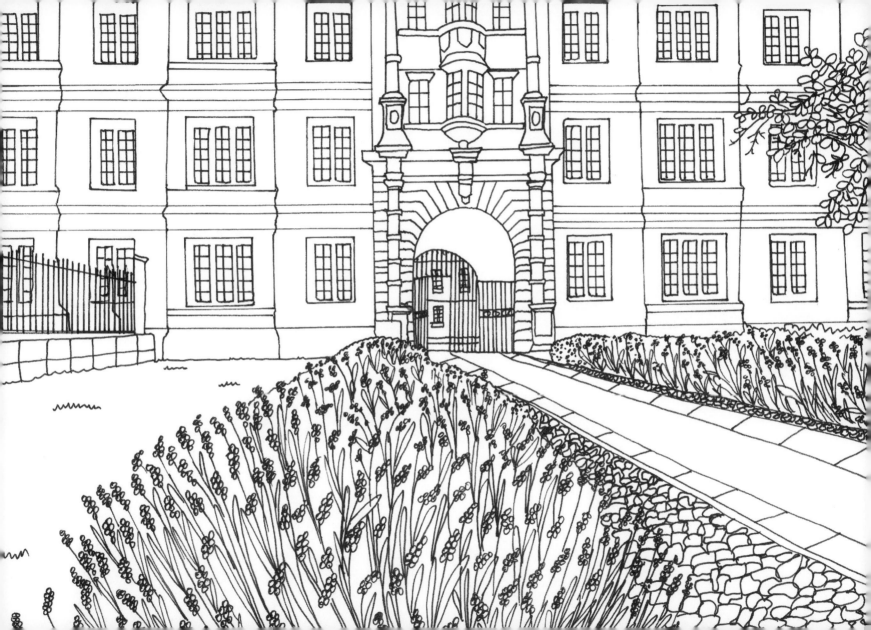

Corpus Christi College, Cambridge ▸

Colourful stained-glass window at the
Stained Glass Museum, Ely Cathedral ▸

St Neots ▶

Elton Hall, Peterborough ▸

Diners enjoy views of the River Ouse, Ely ▸

Great St Mary's Church, Cambridge ▸

H. Russell, grocer, at Broad Street,
March, at the turn of the century ▸

Haida totem pole at the Museum of Archaeology
and Anthropology, University of Cambridge ▸

Market day in Chatteris, 1974 ▶

High Street, Ely, *c.* 1914 ▶

Peckover House, Wisbech ▶

Cambridge Folk Festival ▶

Market Square, Cambridge ▸

Peterborough Cathedral ▶

Punting on the River Cam ▶

Ramsey Abbey, Huntingdon ▶

Rowers on the River Cam ▶

The River Nene at North Brink, Wisbech ▶

Snowy owl at Shepreth Wildlife Park ▸

St Clement's Church, Outwell, in the late 1920s ▶

Steam train at March Station in the 1940s ▶

The Mathematical Bridge,
Queen's College, Cambridge ▸

Sailing at Ferry Meadows Country Park, Peterborough ▸

The Church of the Holy Sepulchre, known as the Round Church, Cambridge ▶

The Backs, Cambridge ▸

Wicken Fen nature reserve ▶

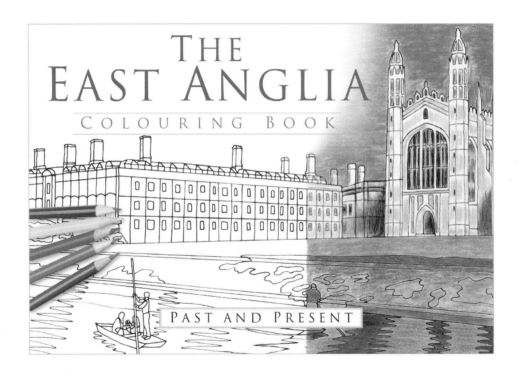